Geek Out!

THE MODERN NERD'S GUIDE TO
TABLETOP AND CARD GAMES

BY JILL KEPPELER

Gareth Stevens
PUBLISHING

Please visit our website, www.garethstevens.com. For a free color catalog of all our high-quality books, call toll free 1-800-542-2595 or fax 1-877-542-2596.

Cataloging-in-Publication Data

Names: Keppeler, Jill.
Title: The modern nerd's guide to tabletop and card games / Jill Keppeler.
Description: New York : Gareth Stevens Publishing, 2018. | Series: Geek out! | Includes index.
Identifiers: LCCN ISBN 9781538212172 (pbk.) | ISBN 9781538212202 (library bound) | ISBN 9781538212196 (6 pack)
Subjects: LCSH: Board games–Juvenile literature. | Card games–Juvenile literature.
Classification: LCC GV1312.K47 2018 | DDC 794–dc23

First Edition

Published in 2018 by
Gareth Stevens Publishing
111 East 14th Street, Suite 349
New York, NY 10003

Copyright © 2018 Gareth Stevens Publishing

Designer: Sarah Liddell
Editor: Joan Stoltman

Photo credits: Cover, p. 1 Oliver Hallmann/Flickr; texture used throughout StrelaStudio/Shutterstock.com; pp. 4, 10, 13 JIP/Wikimedia Commons; p. 5 encierro/Shutterstock.com; p. 8 Creative Lab/Shutterstock.com; p. 9 StanislauV/Shutterstock.com; p. 11 Winger~commonswiki/Wikimedia Commons; p. 12 Bloomberg/Contributor/Bloomberg/Getty Images; p. 15 Daniel Knighton/Contributor/FilmMagic/Getty Images; pp. 17, 26 Justin Sullivan/Getty Images News/Getty Images; p. 19 stockphotofan1/Shutterstock.com; p. 20 Newscast Contributor/Universal Images Group/Getty Images; p. 21 camilla$$/Shutterstock.com; p. 23 Portland Press Herald/Contributor/Portland Press Herald/Getty Images; p. 27 Clarence Williams/Contributor/Los Angeles Times/Getty Images; p. 29 LightField Studios/Shutterstock.com.

Printed in the United States of America

CPSIA compliance information: Batch #CW18GS: For further information contact Gareth Stevens, New York, New York at 1-800-542-2595.

CONTENTS

Words in the glossary appear in **bold** type the first time they are used in the text.

GAME ON!

As the sun rises on a new day here on your island, you have an important decision to make. Do you continue working on the new ship you've been building? Do you go to the market to trade for cool things like gold or tools? Or do you join an attack on a nearby ship?

What if your decision depends on a roll of the **dice** or the draw of a card?

This is the kind of play that might happen while you're playing a tabletop game! Are you ready for all kinds of adventure?

In order to play some tabletop games, you need to use your imagination because you'll be pretending to be a **wizard** or warrior during the game!

ORIGIN STORY

More than 5,000 years ago, the ancient Egyptians played a tabletop game called senet. Some people still play it today, but more people play another very old game: chess! This game—played with pieces called kings, queens, knights, bishops, rooks, and pawns—was first played in India about 1,400 years ago.

Tabletop games are games with pieces that are placed on a flat surface, such as a table. Today, tabletop gaming is a very popular hobby. You've probably played tabletop games before. Popular board games such as Candy Land, checkers, Clue, and Monopoly are all tabletop games! So are card games, like Go Fish and Uno. There are hundreds more games that you've never heard of because new games are being invented regularly.

Role-playing games (RPGs), dice games, tile-based games, and miniature, or small-scale, games are also considered tabletop games. What type of game might be right for you?

SNAKES OR CHUTES?

Since around 200 BC, people in India have played the game snakes and ladders, moving their pieces up the board on ladders and down the board on snakes. Does this sound familiar? Today, this game is Chutes and Ladders, which the Milton Bradley Company first produced in the United States in 1943.

TABLETOP TIMELINE

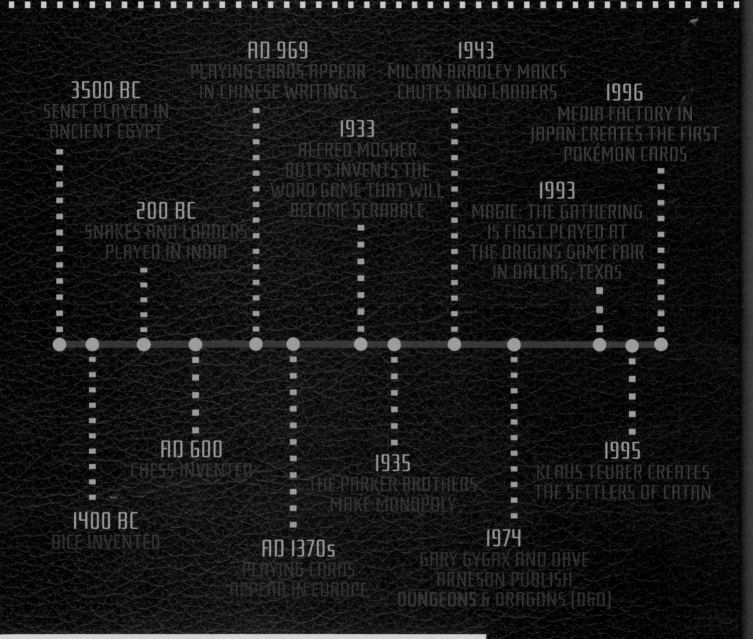

3500 BC
SENET PLAYED IN
ANCIENT EGYPT

AD 969
PLAYING CARDS APPEAR
IN CHINESE WRITINGS

1943
MILTON BRADLEY MAKES
CHUTES AND LADDERS

1996
MEDIA FACTORY IN
JAPAN CREATES THE FIRST
POKÉMON CARDS

1933
ALFRED MOSHER
BUTTS INVENTS THE
WORD GAME THAT WILL
BECOME SCRABBLE

200 BC
SNAKES AND LADDERS
PLAYED IN INDIA

1993
MAGIC: THE GATHERING
IS FIRST PLAYED AT
THE ORIGINS GAME FAIR
IN DALLAS, TEXAS

AD 600
CHESS INVENTED

1935
THE PARKER BROTHERS
MAKE MONOPOLY

1995
KLAUS TEUBER CREATES
THE SETTLERS OF CATAN

1400 BC
DICE INVENTED

AD 1370s
PLAYING CARDS
APPEAR IN EUROPE

1974
GARY GYGAX AND DAVE
ARNESON PUBLISH
DUNGEONS & DRAGONS (D&D)

There's a lot of history behind tabletop games.
From the first-known board game to the first
Pokémon cards, here are some important dates.

GAMES, GAMES, AND MORE GAMES!

Whether you're only interested in card games or will play anything with a history theme, there are so many tabletop games that there's truly something for everyone. The website BoardGameGeek.com lists over 92,000 games in 84 **categories**! Categories on BoardGameGeek.com range from adventure games to **zombie** games. It's all about trying new things until you find what you love.

There are themes that show up throughout all the types of tabletop gaming. Just using the example of ghosts, there's a **cooperative** board game (Ghost Stories), a card game (Ghost Blitz), a mystery board game (Mysterium), and a two-player miniature game (Ghosts).

There can be some overlap in game types. Both dice and cards are used in many board games. You also use dice or have a board in some role-playing games.

LOTS OF VARIETY

Some of the most popular games take their themes from famous movies, television, and books. The worlds of Star Wars, *The Lord of the Rings*, *The Simpsons*, Harry Potter, and Marvel Comics can all be found in the tabletop gaming world. There are games for people who love cats, words, riddles, love stories, and crimes, too!

ARE YOU READY?

On the box, most game companies list the suggested age at which people can start playing a game. However, even if a game isn't suggested for your age, you might be able to play with the help of an adult. After all, it's just a suggestion!

Also, some popular games, such as Ticket to Ride, Carcassonne, Five Crowns, and Stone Age, have **versions** just for younger people. Catan Junior is suggested for people ages 6 and older. Apples to Apples Junior is for ages 9 and up. Trivial Pursuit: Family Edition is for ages 8 and older.

> It can be a lot of fun to learn new games as a family. You can even read the rules ahead of time to help out!

CARCASSONNE

THE SETTLERS OF CATAN

The Settlers of Catan—now just called Catan—is one of the most popular board games today. In this game, players work with and against each other to build roads and communities on a beautiful island. People have bought more than 18 million copies of the game since it first came out in 1995!

ON THE BOARD

A tabletop game is called a board game if you play it by moving pieces on a board. Many board games have other parts, though. In Monopoly, for example, there are cards to collect and others to draw, as well as dice, money, pieces, and buildings.

Many tabletop games involve players battling against each other. The goal could be to be the first to reach the end of the board or to have the most land or money at the end of the game. In some tabletop games, however, players work *together* to build communities, create businesses, fight monsters, solve mysteries, cure sicknesses, or more!

There's even a world championship tournament for Catan. The event is held every other year.

WHAT'S AN EXPANSION?

You can buy expansions for many board games. An expansion includes extra supplies that add to the game. It might make it possible to take part in a new story, add more players, or change the rules of the game! The railroad-building board game Ticket to Ride, for example, has two expansions: USA 1910 and Europa 1912.

PLAYING A ROLE

In RPGs, or role-playing games, each player takes on the role of a character. You can create this character yourself and give them a story and skills. Then, you play as the character during the game's story, which is usually guided by a leader called a game master (GM).

Many say that Dungeons & Dragons is the most famous RPG. Players go on adventures in a **fantasy** world. Have you ever wanted to slay—or even make friends with—a dragon? Do you think it'd be fun to cast spells as a wizard? Here's your chance! Plus, there are many different versions of D&D.

CHARACTERS AND CREATURES

It can be a ton of fun to create a D&D character. Your character could be a human, an elf, a dwarf, or another type of adventurer. You'll also decide if your character will be a fighter, a wizard, a ruler, or one of the many other roles!

D&D and other role-playing games are all about storytelling and imagination. You have to think about how your character—not you—would act during the events of the game. If a dragon charges at you, will you run away or swing your sword?

D&D

IN THE CARDS

Have you ever played Go Fish or War before? If so, you've done it with a standard deck of cards. These have four suits and two joker cards, which can be left out depending on the game being played.

Collectible card games (CCGs) are card games where players put together their own deck of cards with which to play the game. This can be done by trading or buying cards. Each card has special powers and abilities. The Pokémon card game is a very popular CCG. With Pokémon and other CCGs, part of the fun is collecting the cards!

MAGIC: THE GATHERING

Magic: The Gathering was the first modern CCG. In this fantasy card game, players battle each other as Planeswalkers, characters with the ability to travel between worlds. Today, there are more than 12,000 cards for this game in 11 languages. More than 12 million people around the world play it!

TRAINER

Battle Compressor Team Flare Gear

An important part of many types of tabletop and card games is **strategy**. It's not just about what cards you have, it's about how you play them.

ROLLING THE DICE

Players have to roll dice in many games, but in some, it's the most important part of the game. Some popular dice games include Yahtzee, Farkle, and Zombie Dice. King of Tokyo, which includes dice and cards, lets you control a monster as it fights other monsters and takes control of a city!

Luck and chance play a bigger role in dice games. It often doesn't take as much strategy to play them, so they can be easier to learn. They also tend to be quicker, so you don't need a lot of time to play a whole game!

SO MANY SIDES

Some games use the common, six-sided, cube-shaped dice, but other games need special dice. Dungeons & Dragons uses a set of seven dice, including 4-sided, 6-sided, 8-sided, 10-sided, 12-sided, and 20-sided dice. This set is often used in other RPGs, too. Gaming dice are usually made of plastic, though metal, wood, bone, and glass dice can be found, too!

A four-sided die is called a d4, a six-sided die is called a d6, and so on. Many dice games have their own special dice, however. DICEcapades is a board game that includes 50 dice of all shapes and sizes!

TINY ARMIES

All tabletop games use some sort of pieces, but miniature games have very special ones. The games themselves aren't small, but they're played with pieces that are miniature models of characters and features in the game. These games may be played in handmade miniature worlds on tabletops.

Many miniature games are war games, in which players' tiny armies battle other players' tiny armies. They may be set in historic war situations or in fantasy or space battles. Players often take great care in painting their miniatures or building their playing surface. That's part of the fun of the game!

One popular miniature game is Warhammer. There are a number of versions of this fantasy game.

PUTTING THE PIECES TOGETHER

Tile-based games also have important pieces, although they're not as **unique** as those in miniature games. Scrabble tiles have letters. Domino tiles have dots. Mah-jongg tiles have **symbols**. Rummikub tiles have numbers. Tiles can also be found in board games like Catan, Tsuro, and Forbidden Island.

LET'S GET IT STARTED!

Tabletop and card games can be expensive, so it's important to "try before you buy." Luckily, there are several ways you can try out games first! Some communities have gaming groups that meet to play games together. You might be able to find these groups through your library or have your parents search for gaming events or groups for kids your age. Your local game shop is also a great place to try out new games!

Remember when you're trying out games that just because one card game isn't for you, it doesn't mean that you won't like *all* card games.

LOCAL GAMING SHOPS

People who work at local game shops or comic book stores are great sources to answer all your gaming questions. They can suggest their favorite games to you and tell you why they didn't like playing certain games, too. Game shops often host gaming nights and events where you can meet new friends and try new games!

Gaming can be a good way to meet new friends. If you're interested in playing the same games, you already have something in common!

23

LEARNING A GAME

Some games have a lot of rules. Sometimes, even if there aren't a lot of rules, the rules can seem tough at first. This might make playing the game for the first time, or first few times, a little long. Just remember that after learning the rules, it'll be easier, quicker—and definitely more fun—each time you play!

Once you've learned how to play a game, the fun really begins! There are always new versions of games to learn and strategies to perfect. Plus, now you can teach people to play and maybe even get your friends interested in your favorite game.

TIME TO PLAY!

The amount of time it takes to play a tabletop game can vary widely. Role-playing games such as Dungeons & Dragons can take 3 to 6 hours at a time. It may take days to play a full campaign! Some dice games take only minutes to play. Most games will fall somewhere in the middle.

TIPS FOR HOSTING A GAME NIGHT!

1

SOME GAME NIGHTS ARE ORGANIZED AROUND ONE GAME THAT EVERYONE INVITED IS INTERESTED IN, OR SET OUT SEVERAL GAMES AND CHOOSE TOGETHER WHEN EVERYONE ARRIVES. YOU CAN EVEN HAVE EVERYONE BRING THEIR FAVORITE GAME!

2

AT FIRST, PICK GAMES THAT ARE EASY TO LEARN AND THAT YOU KNOW THE RULES TO.

3

MANY GAMES REQUIRE A CERTAIN NUMBER OF PEOPLE TO PLAY, SO MAKE SURE TO INVITE THE RIGHT NUMBER OF PEOPLE.

4

YOU'LL NEED SNACKS! ASK PEOPLE TO BRING THEIR OWN OR ASK YOUR PARENTS TO HELP OUT.

5

HAVE A TABLE CLEARED AND READY TO PLAY. BE SURE THERE ARE ENOUGH CHAIRS FOR EVERYONE!

Don't forget to ask your parents first if it's okay to invite some friends over for a game night.

PROS

If you get really good at gaming, find out if you can take part in a gaming tournament. Many local game stores host these events and often include chances for younger players to compete. The best players may go on to play in championship contests!

There are world championship tournaments for many games, including Catan, Magic: The Gathering, and the Pokémon card game. Star players can win a lot of money. The winner of the Magic: The Gathering Pro Tour takes home $50,000—that could buy a lot of cards!

POKÉMON WORLD CHAMPIONSHIP

People have to be invited to compete in the Magic: The Gathering Pro Tour. It's only for the best of the best!

CONS

Science fiction, fantasy, and comics **conventions**, or cons, are other good places to learn more about tabletop gaming. Cons often feature a room where people can stop to try out new and old games alike and play against other visitors. Cons also usually have tabletop gaming tournaments!

GO FORTH AND GAME!

Tabletop gaming has been rising in popularity over the past several years. In 2015, more than $1 billion in games were sold in North America alone! Gaming tournaments and conventions are also on the rise.

Now that you've taken a peek into the fun and exciting world of tabletop gaming, it's time to go forth and try it for yourself! If you try one game and don't like it, don't worry. There are other games out there you will like. There are so many different types of games. It's a great time to be a gamer!

HEALTHY HOBBY

Tabletop gaming can be good for you! It helps you learn to think in a creative way and master problem-solving skills. Role-playing games encourage reading and can show you how to tell a good story. Gaming can teach teamwork and give you chances to make new friends.

It doesn't matter if you start with a simple game. What matters is that you give it a try!

GLOSSARY

category: class or group

convention: a gathering of people who have a common interest or purpose

cooperative: involving two or more people or groups working together to do something

dice: small, multisided gaming pieces that have dots on their sides and are rolled to play certain games. One piece is called a "die."

dungeon: a dark prison, usually underground

fantasy: a kind of story involving magic and adventure

role: a part or function

strategy: a plan of action to complete a goal

symbol: a picture that is used instead of a word or group of words

tournament: a series of contests that involves many players or teams and that usually continues for at least several days

unique: unlike anything or anyone else

version: a form of something that is different from other forms

wizard: a person who has magic powers

zombie: in fiction, a dead person who has been turned into a creature capable of movement that feeds on human flesh

FOR MORE INFORMATION

BOOKS

Ho, Oliver. *The Ultimate Book of Family Card Games*. New York City, NY: Sterling Children's Books, 2013.

Ives, Rob. *Castle Attack: Make Your Own Medieval Battlefield*. Minneapolis, MN: Hungry Tomato, 2016.

Scholastic. *Pokémon Classic Collector's Handbook: An Official Guide to the First 151 Pokémon*. New York, NY: Scholastic Inc., 2016.

WEBSITES

Catan Junior
catan.com/game/catan-junior
This web page gives information about Catan Junior.

D&D Lore
dnd.wizards.com/lore
Learn more about the fantasy worlds of D&D.

Pokedex
pokemon.com/us/pokedex/
Look through a list of all the Pokémon cards there are. (There are a lot!)

Publisher's note to educators and parents: Our editors have carefully reviewed these websites to ensure that they are suitable for students. Many websites change frequently, however, and we cannot guarantee that a site's future contents will continue to meet our high standards of quality and educational value. Be advised that students should be closely supervised whenever they access the Internet.

INDEX